LEVEL 5 Supplemental

EXAM SERIES ANSWERS

By Glory St. Germain ARCT RMT MYCC UMTC &
Shelagh McKibbon-U'Ren RMT UMTC

ULTIMATE
MUSIC THEORY

GSG MUSIC

Enriching Lives Through Music Education

ISBN: 978-1-990358-12-8

The Ultimate Music Theory™ Program

Enriching Lives Through Music Education

The Ultimate Music Theory™ Workbooks & Answer Books Program includes:

UMT Rudiments Workbooks for Prep 1, Prep 2, Basic, Intermediate, Advanced & Complete
UMT Exam Series (Set #1 & Set #2) for Preparatory, Basic, Intermediate & Advanced

Supplemental Workbooks for PREP LEVEL, LEVELS 1 - 8 & COMPLETE LEVEL
UMT Supplemental Exam Series for LEVEL 5, LEVEL 6, LEVEL 7 & LEVEL 8

The Ultimate Music Theory Program is the *Way to Score Success* as UMT helps students prepare for nationally recognized theory examinations including the Royal Conservatory of Music.

Library and Archives Canada Cataloguing in Publication. UMT Workbooks & Exam Series /Glory St. Germain & Shelagh McKibbon-U'Ren. Respect Copyright. All rights reserved. GlorylandPublishing.com

Ultimate Music Theory Rudiments Exam Series

GP - EPS1	ISBN: 978-1-927641-00-2	Preparatory Rudiments Exams Set #1
GP - EPS1A	ISBN: 978-1-927641-08-8	Preparatory Exams Answers Set #1
GP - EPS2	ISBN: 978-1-927641-01-9	Preparatory Rudiments Exams Set #2
GP - EPS2A	ISBN: 978-1-927641-09-5	Preparatory Exams Answers Set #2
GP - EBS1	ISBN: 978-1-927641-02-6	Basic Rudiments Exams Set #1
GP - EBS1A	ISBN: 978-1-927641-10-1	Basic Exams Answers Set #1
GP - EBS2	ISBN: 978-1-927641-03-3	Basic Rudiments Exams Set #2
GP - EBS2A	ISBN: 978-1-927641-11-8	Basic Exams Answers Set #2
GP - EIS1	ISBN: 978-1-927641-04-0	Intermediate Rudiments Exams Set #1
GP - EIS1A	ISBN: 978-1-927641-12-5	Intermediate Exams Answers Set #1
GP - EIS2	ISBN: 978-1-927641-05-7	Intermediate Rudiments Exams Set #2
GP - EIS2A	ISBN: 978-1-927641-13-2	Intermediate Exams Answers Set #2
GP - EAS1	ISBN: 978-1-927641-06-4	Advanced Rudiments Exams Set #1
GP - EAS1A	ISBN: 978-1-927641-14-9	Advanced Exams Answers Set #1
GP - EAS2	ISBN: 978-1-927641-07-1	Advanced Rudiments Exams Set #2
GP - EAS2A	ISBN: 978-1-927641-15-6	Advanced Exams Answers Set #2

Ultimate Music Theory Supplemental Exam Series

GP-L5E	ISBN: 978-1-990358-11-1	LEVEL 5 Exams
GP-L5EA	ISBN: 978-1-990358-12-8	LEVEL 5 Exams Answers
GP-L6E	ISBN: 978-1-990358-13-5	LEVEL 6 Exams
GP-L6EA	ISBN: 978-1-990358-14-2	LEVEL 6 Exams Answers
GP-L7E	ISBN: 978-1-990358-15-9	LEVEL 7 Exams
GP-L7EA	ISBN: 978-1-990358-16-6	LEVEL 7 Exams Answers
GP-L8E	ISBN: 978-1-990358-17-3	LEVEL 8 Exams
GP-L8EA	ISBN: 978-1-990358-18-0	LEVEL 8 Exams Answers

Go to UltimateMusicTheory.com and check out the FREE Resources

Ultimate Music Theory FREE RESOURCES created just for you!

Ultimate Music Theory
LEVEL 5 Supplemental Exams

Table of Contents

Score: 60 - 69 Pass; **70 - 79** Honors; **80 - 89** First Class Honors; **90 - 100** First Class Honors with Distinction

Ultimate Music Theory: *The Way to Score Success!*

The 2016 Royal Conservatory of Music Theory Syllabus additional concepts to the Level 5 (formerly the Basic Rudiments) Examination Requirements include:

♫ **Rhythm and Meter**: New Time Signature: $\frac{6}{8}$ (Time Signatures, Bar Lines, Notes and Rests).

♫ **Scales**: Parallel Major and minor keys (up to 4 sharps and 4 flats).
   Scale Degree Names: Tonic, Subdominant, Dominant, Leading Tone and Subtonic.

♫ **Chords and Harmony**: Tonic, Subdominant and Dominant triads in Root Position and Inversions.
   Dominant 7th Chords in Root Position.
   Functional Chord Symbols (I, i, IV, iv, V, V7) in Root Position only.
   Root/Quality Chord Symbols (for example, C, Am, G7).

♫ **Melody and Composition**: Composition of a 4 measure answer (consequent) phrase to a given question (antecedent) phrase in a Major key, creating a parallel period.
   Stable and Unstable Scale Degrees.

♫ **Form and Analysis**: Identification of Question-Answer Phrase pairs (parallel period).
   Melodic Phrases: same, similar or different (a, a1 or b).

♫ **Musical Terms and Signs**: New Terms and Signs have been added.

♫ **Music History**: Voices in Song. "Hallelujah Chorus" from Messiah; "Queen of the Night" from The Magic Flute; and "Over the Rainbow" from The Wizard of Oz.

Circle of Fifths

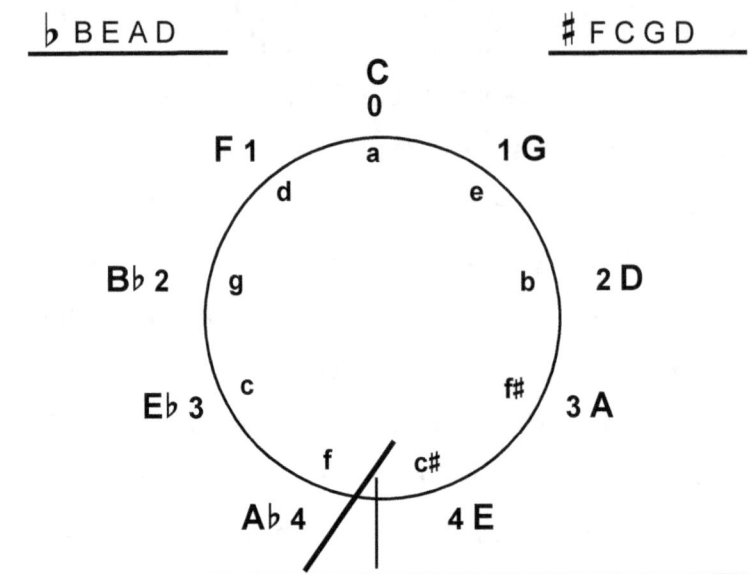

♭ B E A D   ♯ F C G D

C
0

F 1   1 G
  a
 d   e

B♭ 2   g   b   2 D

E♭ 3   c   f#   3 A

       f   c#

A♭ 4   4 E

Keyboard

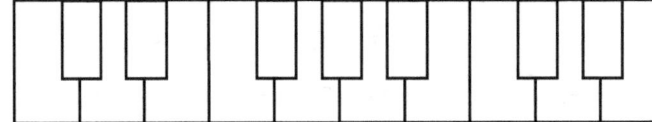

Minor Scales

 N   Natural: Nothing Added

   Harmonic: 7↑

      Melodic: 6 & 7↑ ↓
   6   7

Intervals

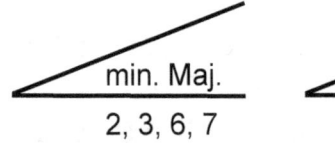 min. Maj.   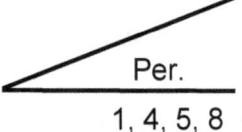 Per.
2, 3, 6, 7   1, 4, 5, 8

Harmonic: tog.

 Melodic: sep.

Degree   ## Triads

	Major	minor
Tonic:	I	i
Subdominant:	IV	iv
Dominant:	V	V (7↑)

V is Always Major - contains the raised 7th
note of the harmonic minor scale

Distances

whole step - equals 2 half steps (semitones)

chromatic half step - same letter name

diatonic half step - different letter name

enharmonic equivalents - same pitch,
                              diff. letter name

Exam Tip: Copy the UMT Map for LEVEL 5 below. Using a blank piece of paper, write out the UMT Map from memory before beginning each practice exam and the final exam.

Circle of Fifths

♭ *BEAD*   ♯ *FCGD*

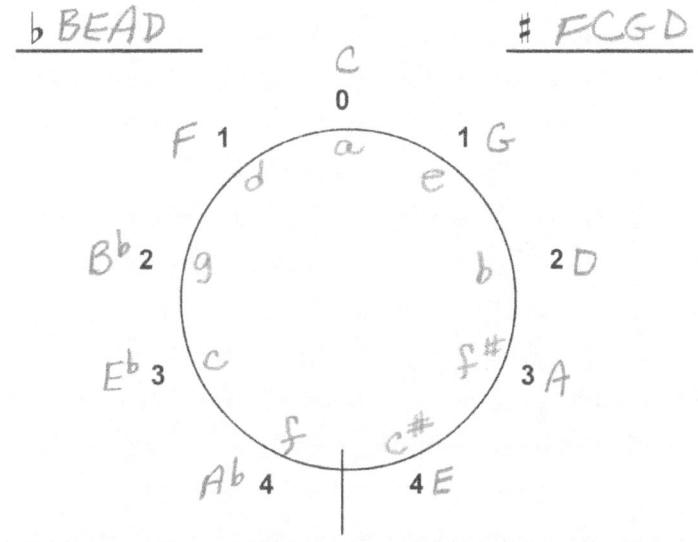

C
0

F 1   *a*   1 G

d   *e*

B♭ 2   *g*   *b*   2 D

E♭ 3   *c*   *f♯*   3 A

f   *c♯*

A♭ 4   4 E

Keyboard

Minor Scales

N   Natural :   Nothing Added

H   Harmonic :   7 ↑

Melodic :   6 + 7 ↑↓

Intervals

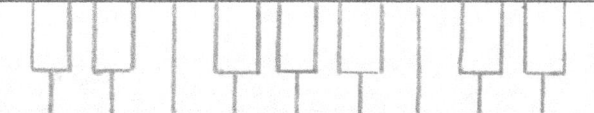

min   Maj   Per
2, 3, 6, 7   1, 4, 5, 8

Harmonic :   tog.

Melodic :   sep.

Degree   Triads

	Major	**minor**
Tonic :	I	i
Subdominant :	IV	iv
Dominant :	V	V (7↑)

V is Always Major - contains the raised 7th
note of the harmonic minor scale

Distances

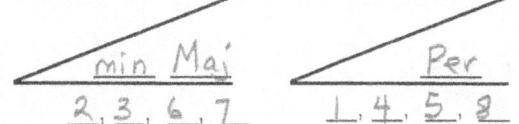

Whole step - equals 2 half steps (semitones)

Chromatic half step - same letter name

diatonic half step - different letter name

enharmonic equivalents - same pitch,
diff. letter name

Ultimate Music Theory
Level 5 Supplemental Exam #1

Use with Basic Exam Set #1 - Exam #1

Total Score: ____
50

The Ultimate Music Theory™ Basic Rudiments Workbook, LEVELS 4 & 5 Supplemental Workbooks, Basic Rudiments Exam Series and Level 5 Supplemental Exams prepare students for successful completion of the Royal Conservatory of Music Level 5 Theory Examination.

1. Write the following Solid (Blocked) Triads and Chords in Root Position. Use whole notes. Use a Key Signature and any necessary accidentals. Write the Root/Quality Chord Symbol above and the Functional Chord Symbol below.

10 a) The Tonic Triad of D Major.
      b) The Subdominant Triad of d minor.
      c) The Dominant Seventh Chord of g minor.
      d) The Dominant Triad of A Major.
      e) The Dominant Seventh Chord of E Major.

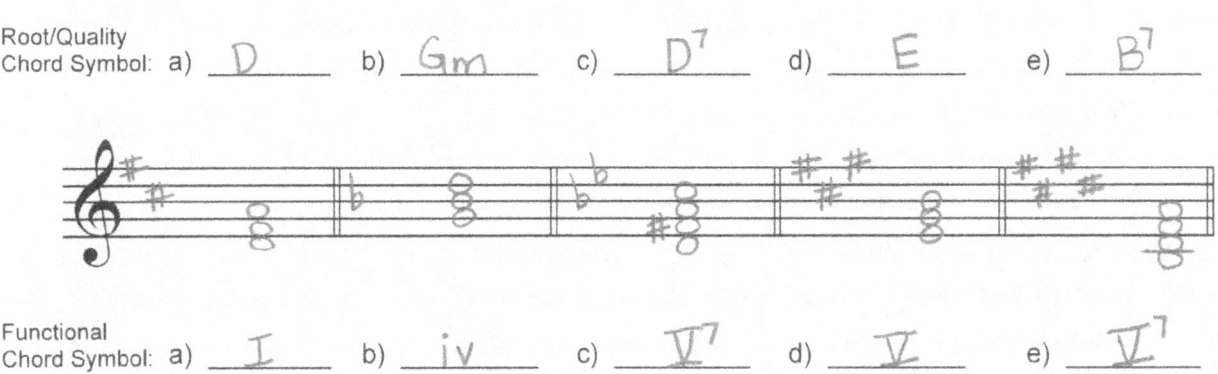

2. Add rests below the brackets to complete each of the following measures.

Ultimate Music Theory
Level 5 Supplemental Exam #1

3. a) Name the key of this melody.
    b) Draw a phrase mark (slur) over the given Question phrase. Label the scale degree number of the final note in the Question phrase.
    c) Compose a four-measure Answer phrase to create a Parallel Period. End on a stable scale degree. (There will be more than one correct answer.)
    d) Draw a phrase mark over the Answer phrase. Label the scale degree number of the final note.

10

Key: G Major

4. Match each musical term or sign with the English definition. (Not all definitions will be used.)

10

Term		Definition
tranquillo	c	a) much, very
spiritoso	i	b) lively, brisk
poco	f	c) quiet, tranquil
rubato	l	d) left hand
molto	a	e) slow
leggiero	j	f) little
vivace	b	g) from the sign
espressivo	k	h) becoming louder
dal segno, D.S.	g	i) spirited
lento	e	j) light, nimble, quick
mano sinistra, m.s.	d	k) with expression, expressive
		l) with some freedom of tempo to enhance musical expression

5.   Answer the following questions.

a) Name the Composer of the "Hallelujah Chorus".

10   G. F. Handel

b) Name the Oratorio that features the "Hallelujah Chorus".

Messiah

c) List the type of voices that sing in the chorus of the "Hallelujah Chorus".

Soprano, Alto, Tenor, Bass

d) Name the Composer of "Over the Rainbow".

Harold Arlen

e) Name the Movie that features "Over the Rainbow".

The Wizard of Oz

f) Name the structure of "Over the Rainbow".

Vocal with Verse-Chorus Structure

g) Name the Composer of "Queen of the Night".

W. A. Mozart

h) Name the Opera that features "Queen of the Night".

The Magic Flute

i) Name the type of voice (voice type) that sings "Queen of the Night".

Coloratura Soprano

j) Name one example of the relationship between text and music in "Queen of the Night".
   (There will be more than one correct answer).

text: Hear a mother's oath (a cappella)   Sound and Silence

text: Go forth and bear (my vengeance)   Dynamics and Articulation

1. Name the scale. Write the scale, ascending and descending, using the correct Key Signature and any necessary accidentals for each. Use whole notes.

____
10

a) The Relative Major scale of c minor is: *Eb Major*   .

b) The Parallel (Tonic) minor scale, melodic form, of G Major is: *g minor melodic*.

c) The Relative minor scale, natural form, of A flat Major is: *f minor natural*   .

d) The Major scale with 3 sharps is: *A Major*   .

e) The Parallel (Tonic) Major scale of e minor is: *E Major*   .

2. Name the Major key and the minor key for each of the following Dominant Seventh Chords.

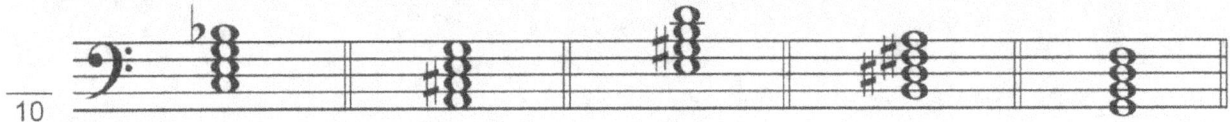

Major key: a) _F Major_   b) _D Major_   c) _A Major_   d) _E Major_   e) _C Major_

minor key: a) _f minor_   b) _d minor_   c) _a minor_   d) _e minor_   e) _c minor_

3. Write the following Solid (Blocked) Triads in the Treble Clef. Use a Key Signature and any necessary accidentals. Use whole notes.

   a) The Dominant Triad of A flat Major, in root position.
   b) The Tonic Triad of e minor, harmonic form, in second inversion.

   10

   c) The Dominant Triad of g minor, harmonic form, in first inversion.
   d) The Subdominant Triad of G Major, in second inversion.
   e) The Subdominant Triad of f minor, harmonic form, in first inversion.

   a)   b)   c)   d)   e)

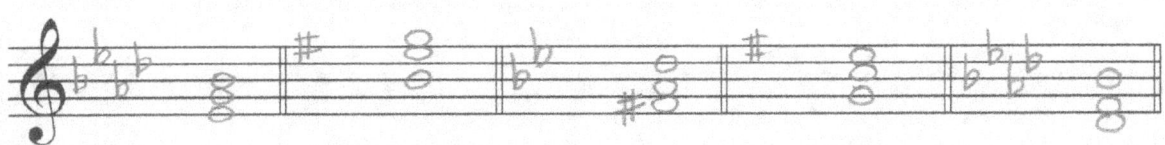

4. Write the definition for each of the following signs.

   a) ,   _breath mark - take a breath and/or slight pause or lift_

   10

   b) ⊓   _down bow - on a bowed string instrument, play the note while drawing the bow downward_

   c) V   _Up bow - on a bowed string instrument, play the note while drawing the bow upward_

   d) 𝄋   _dal segno, D.S., from the sign_

   e) ¢   _cut time or 2/2 time (Alla breve)_

5. For each of the following melodies:

   a) Name the key of the melody.
   b) Mark the two four-measure phrases with a slur.
10 c) Identify each phrase as a, a1 or b.
   d) Answer the questions below each melody by circling TRUE or FALSE.

Melody #1:

Key: A♭ Major

i) TRUE or (FALSE:) Melody #1 is an example of a Parallel Period.

ii) (TRUE) or FALSE: The second phrase in Melody #1 ends on a stable scale degree.

Melody #2:

Key: D Major

iii) (TRUE) or FALSE: Melody #2 is an example of a Parallel Period.

iv) (TRUE) or FALSE: The second phrase in Melody #2 ends on a stable scale degree.

Ultimate Music Theory
LEVEL 5 Supplemental Exam #3

Use with Basic Exam Set #1 - Exam #3

Total Score: _____
50

1. a) Name the key of this melody.
    b) Draw a phrase mark (slur) over the given Question phrase. Label the scale degree number of the final note in the Question phrase.
___ c) Compose a four-measure Answer phrase to create a Parallel Period. End on a stable scale
10   degree. (There will be more than one correct answer.)
    d) Draw a phrase mark over the Answer phrase. Label the scale degree number of the final note.

Key: C Major

2. Write the following Solid (Blocked) Chords or Triads in the Bass Clef. Use accidentals. Use whole notes.

___ a) The Dominant Seventh Chord of A Major in root position.
10 b) The Dominant Triad of b minor harmonic form in second inversion.
    c) The Tonic Triad of g minor harmonic form in first inversion.
    d) The Dominant Seventh Chord of d minor harmonic form in root position.
    e) The Subdominant Triad of B flat Major in second inversion.

a)   b)   c)   d)   e)

3. a) Add rests below the brackets to complete each of the following measures.

b) Add bar lines. Add a double bar line at the end.

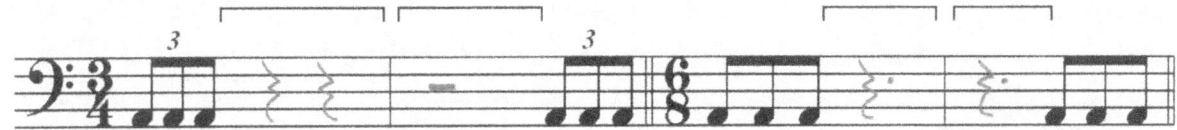

4. Write the term or word that each of the following statements applies to. Use the following terms or words (not all terms and words will be used).

Orchestra   ✓Opera   ✓Genre   ✓Aria   ✓Oratorio   Coloratura   ✓Chorus

10

a) _Genre_ - A classification system used to describe and define the standard category and overall character of a work (form, style, type, period, etc.).

b) _Opera_ - A dramatic production of a story, performed in concert setting, that uses costumes, scenery, singing, acting and action.

c) _Oratorio_ - A production of a Biblical or religious story, performed in a church or concert setting, that does not use costumes, scenery or acting.

d) _Aria_ - A lyric song for solo voice with orchestral accompaniment that expresses intense emotion in the story.

e) _Chorus_ - A large group of singers performing together in various voice parts (including SATB).

5. Analyze this excerpt from Musette in D Major (from the Notebook for Anna Magdalena Bach) by answering the questions below.

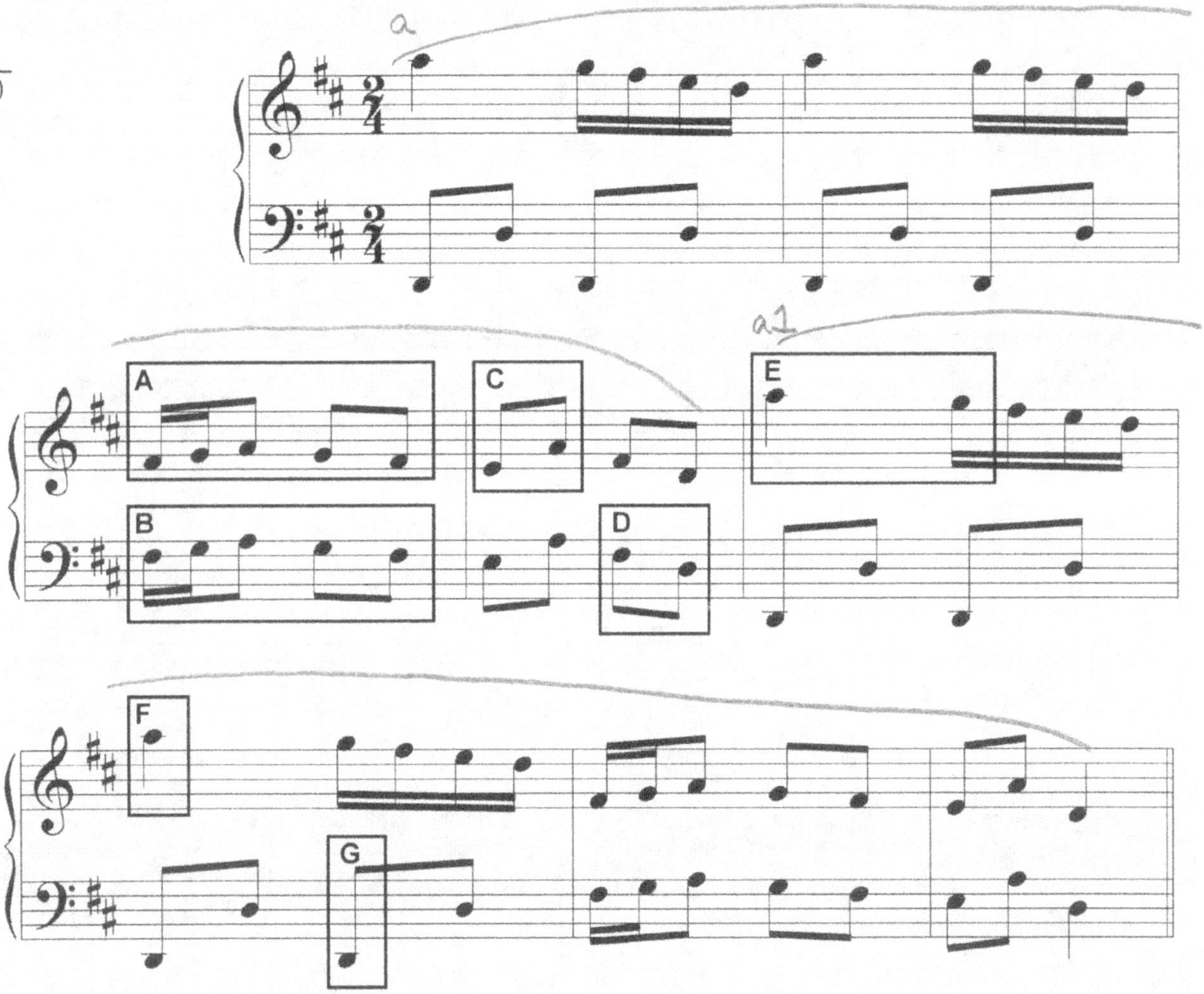

a) Mark the two four-measure phrases directly in this excerpt. Label them as a, a1 or b.

b) Circle if the notes at **A** and at **B** are moving in: (Parallel Motion) or Contrary Motion

c) Identify the intervals at **C**: _Per 4_ ; **D**: _Maj 3_ ; **E**: _Maj 2_

d) Identify the Technical Degree Name of the notes at **F**: _Dominant_ ; **G**: _Tonic_

e) How many times does the rhythmic motive ♩ ♪♪♪♪ appear in this excerpt? _4_

1. Identify the name (term) for each of the following signs.

____
10

a) V   *up bow*

b) ♪   *staccato*

c) ¢   *cut time or alla breve*

d) Ped.   *pedal marking*

e) ,   *breath mark*

f) ♩   *tenuto*

g) 𝄋   *dal segno*

h) ♩   *accent*

i) ⊓   *down bow*

j) 𝄐   *fermata*

2. a) Name the key of this melody.
    b) Draw a phrase mark (slur) over the given Question phrase. Label the scale degree number of the final note in the Question phrase.
    c) Compose a four-measure Answer phrase to create a Parallel Period. End on a stable scale degree. (There will be more than one correct answer.)
    d) Draw a phrase mark over the Answer phrase. Label the scale degree number of the final note.

____
10

Key: *D Major*

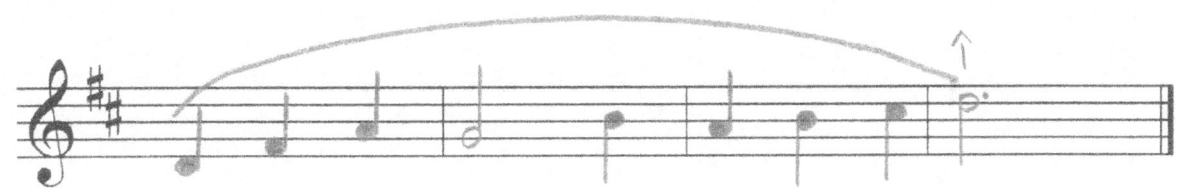

3.   Circle **Correct** if the placement (values) of the rests below the bracket in each measure is correct. Circle **Incorrect** if it is not.

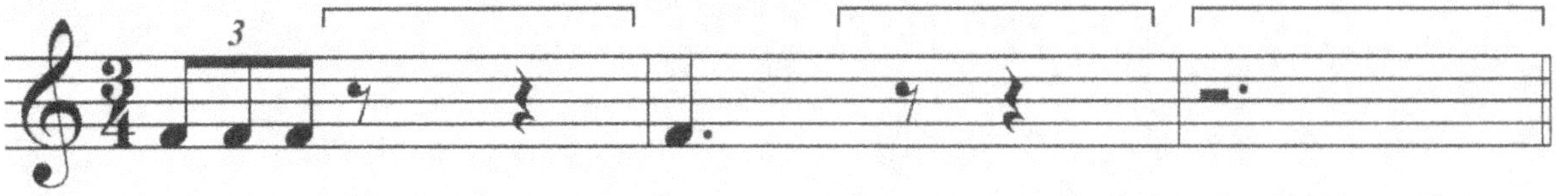

Correct   ~~Correct~~   Correct

~~Incorrect~~   Incorrect   ~~Incorrect~~

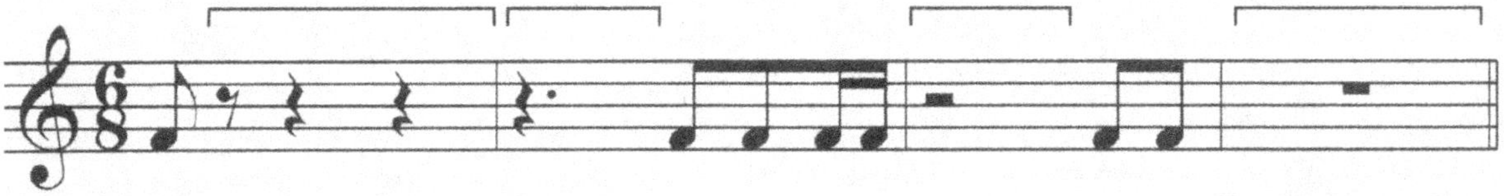

Correct   ~~Correct~~   Correct   ~~Correct~~

~~Incorrect~~   Incorrect   ~~Incorrect~~   Incorrect

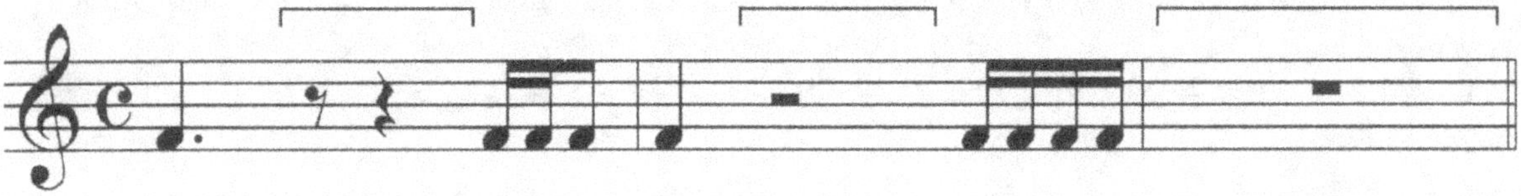

~~Correct~~   Correct   ~~Correct~~

Incorrect   ~~Incorrect~~   Incorrect

4.   Name the key (Major or minor) for each of the following Dominant Seventh Chords.

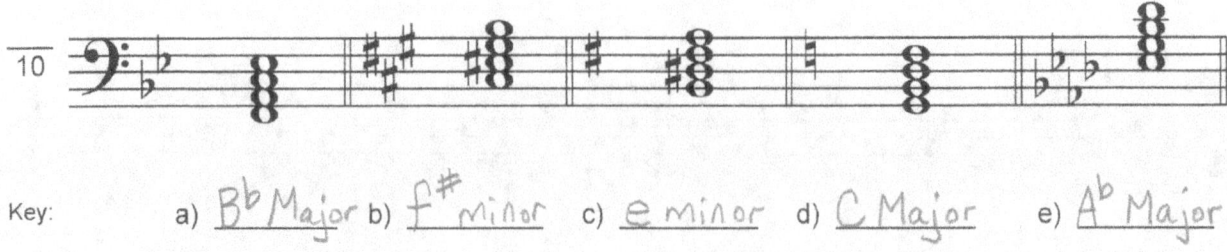

Key: a) B♭ Major b) f♯ minor c) e minor d) C Major e) A♭ Major

5. Analyze this excerpt from Menuet in g minor (from the Notebook for Anna Magdalena Bach) by answering the questions below.

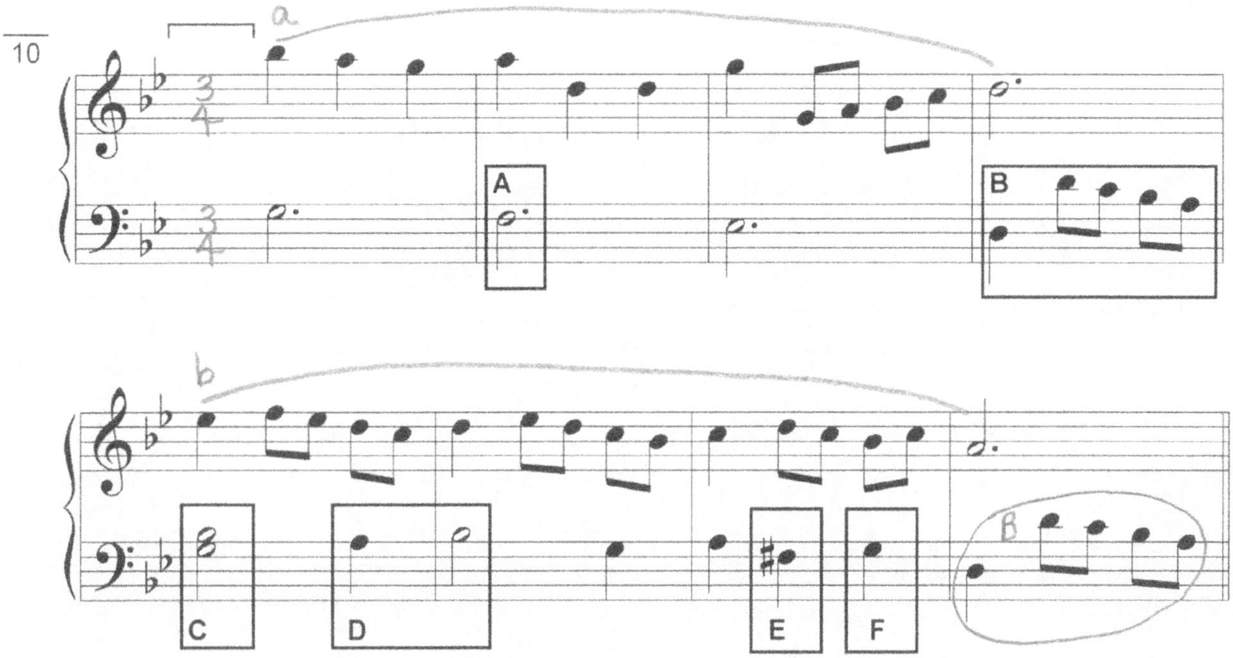

a) Name the key of this excerpt. ___g minor___

b) Write the Time Signature directly on the music.

c) Mark the two four-measure phrases in this excerpt. Label them as a, a1 or b.

d) The technical degree of the note at letter **A** is the: ☐Tonic ☐Subdominant ☑Subtonic.

e) Circle a recurrence of the notes (melodic and rhythmic) at letter **B**.

f) Identify the interval at letter **C**. ___min 3___. This interval is: ☑Harmonic ☐Melodic.

g) Identify the interval at letter **D**. ___min 2___. This interval is: ☐Harmonic ☑Melodic.

h) Identify the Technical Degree Name of the note at letter **E**. ___Leading tone___

i) Identify the Technical Degree Name of the note at letter **F**. ___Tonic___

j) How many times does the rhythmic motive ♩ ♫ ♫ appear in this excerpt? ___6___

1.   Name the Parallel (Tonic) or Relative Major or minor key for each of the following.

___ / 10

a) The Parallel (Tonic) Major key of g minor. *G Major*

b) The Relative Major key of f sharp minor. *A Major*

c) The Relative minor key of A flat Major. *f minor*

d) The Parallel (Tonic) minor key of D Major. *d minor*

e) The Parallel (Tonic) Major key of a minor. *A Major*

f) The Relative minor key of A Major. *f# minor*

g) The Relative Major key of a minor. *C Major*

h) The Parallel (Tonic) Major key of f minor. *F Major*

i) The Relative minor key of B flat Major. *g minor*

j) The Parallel (Tonic) minor key of C Major. *c minor*

2.   a) Name the key of this melody.
   b) Draw a phrase mark (slur) over the given Question phrase. Label the scale degree number of the final note in the Question phrase.
   c) Compose a four-measure Answer phrase to create a Parallel Period. End on a stable scale degree. (There will be more than one correct answer.)
   d) Draw a phrase mark over the Answer phrase. Label the scale degree number of the final note.

___ / 10

Key: *C Major*

3.   Rewrite the following rhythms beaming the notes correctly.

10

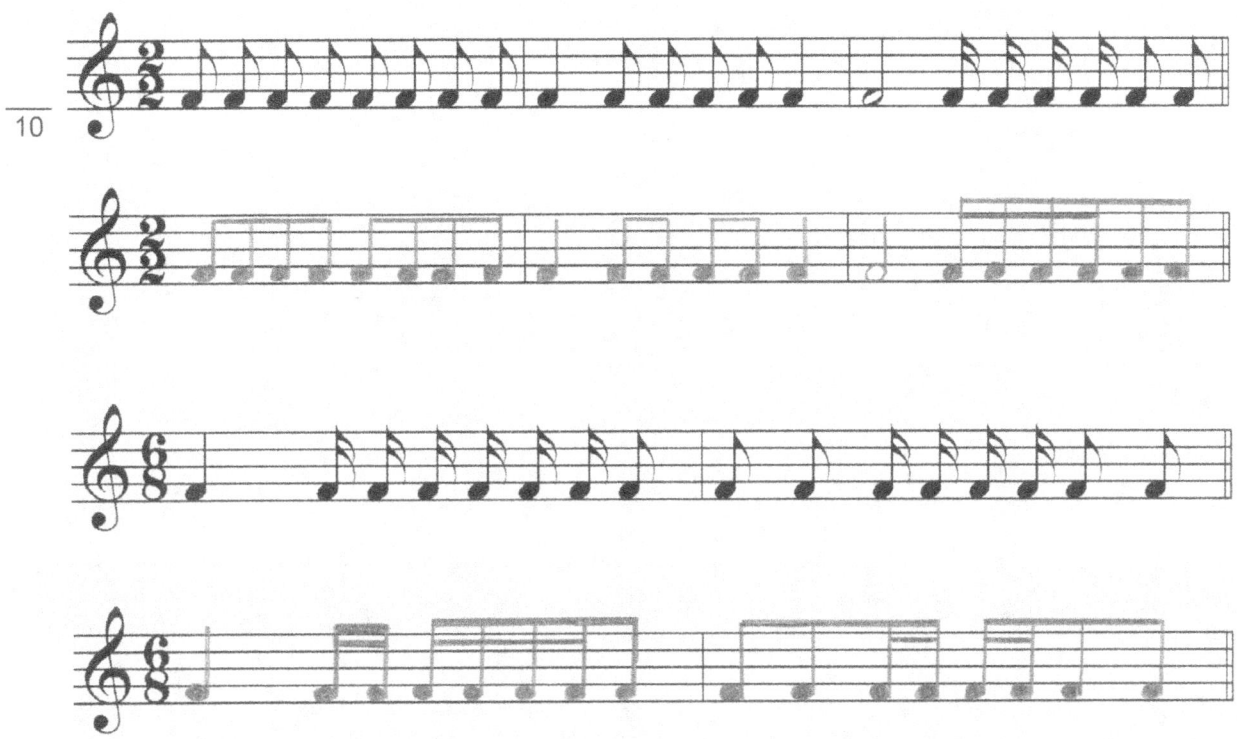

4.   Write the term or word that each of the following statements applies to. Use the following terms or words (not all terms and words will be used):

Coloratura   Aria   Performing Forces   Libretto   Verse-Chorus Structure   Word Painting

10

a)   Performing Forces _____ - This term is used to describe or indicate the instruments or voice types used to perform a work, a piece or a song.

b)   Verse-Chorus Structure - A type of Vocal Music in which each stanza develops the story line and each refrain is repeated at the end of each stanza.

c)   Coloratura (Soprano) _____ - A type of dramatic and powerful Soprano voice that is highly agile, trained to specialize in large vocal leaps, trills, arpeggios, etc.

d)   Word Painting _____ - A musical technique that specifically refers to when the music reflects the literal meaning of the text.

e)   Libretto _____ - An Italian Term meaning a "little book", it is the text of the story of an Oratorio or an Opera.

5.   For each of the following melodies:

   a) Name the key of the melody.
   b) Mark the two four-measure phrases with a slur.
   c) Identify each phrase as a, a1 or b.
   d) Answer the questions below each melody by circling TRUE or FALSE.

___
10

Melody #1:

Key: _A Major_

i) (TRUE)   or   FALSE: Melody #1 is an example of a Parallel Period.

ii) (TRUE)   or   FALSE: The second phrase in Melody #1 ends on a stable scale degree.

Melody #2:

Key: _f# minor_

iii) TRUE   or   (FALSE)   Melody #2 is an example of a Parallel Period.

iv) (TRUE)   or   FALSE: The second phrase in Melody #2 ends on a stable scale degree.

Ultimate Music Theory
Level 5 Supplemental Exam #6
Use with Basic Exam Set 2 - Exam #2

Total Score: ____

50

1. Write the following Solid (Blocked) Chords or Triads in the given Staff. Use accidentals. Use whole notes.

10   a)   C   b)   Cm   c)   A   d)   Am   e)   C7

f)   D7   g)   A7   h)   Dm   i)   D   j)   G7

2. Add the correct Time Signature under each bracket to complete the following rhythms.

10

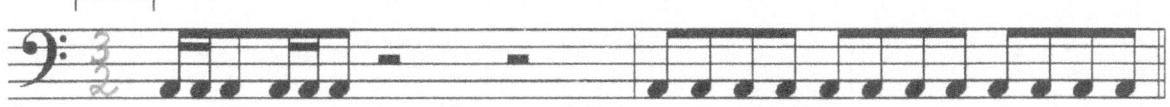

3. Add the following Articulation Signs to the notes as directed.

   a) In measure 1, add a slur above the 4 notes.
   b) In measure 2, add an accent sign to each note.
   c) In measure 3, add a staccato sign to each note.
   10 d) In measure 4, add a tenuto sign to each note.
   e) In measure 5, add a fermata.

4. Identify the work to which each of the following statements applies by writing the appropriate letter (A, B or C) in the space before each statement.

   A - Hallelujah Chorus
   B - Queen of the Night
   10 C - Over the Rainbow

   a) _B_ This work is featured in an opera by W.A. Mozart.

   b) _A_ This work is featured in an oratorio by G.F. Handel.

   c) _C_ This work is a song by Harold Arlen.

   d) _A_ This work is a chorus from "Messiah".

   e) _A_ This work was written for Soprano, Alto, Tenor and Bass voices.

   f) _B_ This work is performed by a Coloratura Soprano voice.

   g) _C_ This work is featured in the movie "The Wizard of Oz".

   h) _B_ This work expresses the character's desire for revenge.

   i) _C_ This work expresses the character's longings and dreams for her life to be different.

   j) _A_ This work expresses the majestic joy at the resurrection of Jesus Christ.

5. Analyze this excerpt from the Trio (from Beethoven's Minuet and Trio in G Major) by answering the questions below.

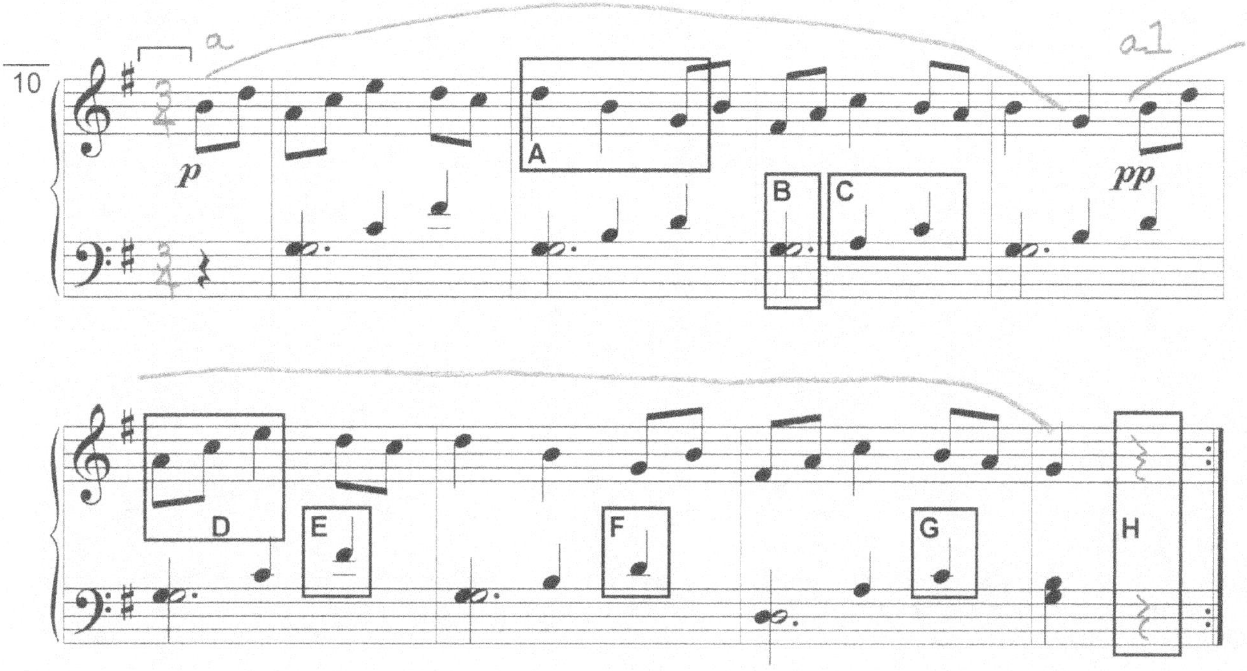

a) Name the key of this excerpt. _G Major_

b) Write the Time Signature directly on the music.

c) Mark the two four-measure phrases in this excerpt. Label them as a, a1 or b.

d) The triad at letter **A** is the: ☑ Tonic Triad ☐ Subdominant Triad ☐ Dominant Triad.

e) Identify the interval at letter **B**. _Per 1_. This interval is: ☑ Harmonic ☐ Melodic.

f) Identify the interval at letter **C**. _min 3_. This interval is: ☐ Harmonic ☑ Melodic.

g) Identify the quality/type of the triad at **D**. _minor_. This triad is: ☐ Solid ☑ Broken.

h) Identify the notes at: **E:** _F#_ ; **F:** _D_ ; **G:** _C_ .

i) Add the missing rest(s) in the box at **H**.

j) Explain the bar line at the end of this excerpt. _repeat signs - repeat the music_

Ultimate Music Theory
Level 5 Supplemental Exam #7

Use with Basic Exam Set 2 - Exam #3

Total Score: ____
                50

1. For each line, name the Key. Write the Solid (Blocked) Chords or Triads in the given Staff. Use accidentals if necessary. Use whole notes.

Key: A Major

Functional
Chord Symbol: a)   I   b)   IV   c)   V   d)   V⁷

Key: g minor

Functional
Chord Symbol: e)   i   f)   iv   g)   V   h)   V⁷

2. Add bar lines to complete the following rhythms. Add a double (final) bar line at the end.

3. Provide an answer (the term or the sign) for each of the following.

    a) A term that means "little": *poco*

10 b) A term that means "much, very": *molto*

    c) A sign that means to take a breath and/or slight lift: 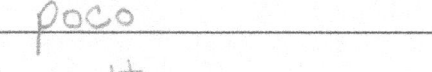 *breath mark*

    d) A sign that means to play detached: *staccato*

    e) A term that means lively, brisk: *Vivace*

    f) A term that means quiet, tranquil: *Tranquillo*

    g) A term that means to play light, nimble, quick: *leggiero*

    h) A term that means expressive, with expression: *espressivo, espress.*

    i) A sign that, on a bowed string instrument, means to
        play the note while drawing the bow upward:  *V up bow*

    j) A sign that, on a bowed string instrument, means to
        play the note while drawing the bow downward: *⊓ down bow*

4. Write the following notes. Use a Key Signature and any necessary accidentals. Use half notes.

    a) The Leading Tone (Leading Note) of c minor.

10 b) The Subtonic of d minor.

    c) The Dominant of B flat Major.

    d) The Subdominant of e minor.

    e) The Leading Tone (Leading Note) of E Major.

    a)   b)   c)   d)   e)

5. Analyze this excerpt from Beethoven's German Dance in G Major by answering the questions below.

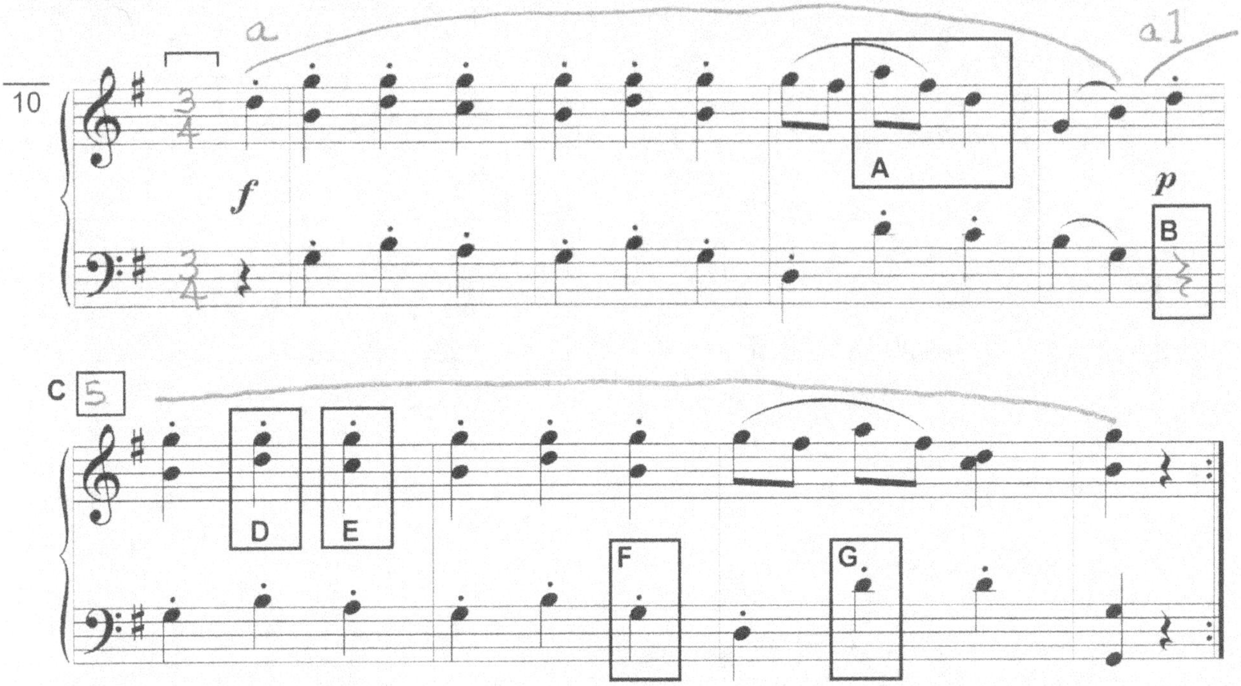

a) Name the key of this excerpt. _G Major_

b) Write the Time Signature directly on the music.

c) Mark the two four-measure phrases in this excerpt. Label them as a, a1 or b.

d) The triad at letter **A** is the: ☐ Tonic Triad ☐ Subdominant Triad ☑ Dominant Triad.

e) Add the correct rest at letter **B**. Identify the type of rest used. _quarter rest_

f) Add the measure number at letter **C**.

g) Identify the interval at letter **D**. _Per 4_. Identify the interval at letter **E**. _Per 5_.

h) Identify the Technical Degree Name of the note at: **F**: _Tonic_.

i) Identify the Technical Degree Name of the note at: **G**: _Dominant_.

j) When played, how many measures are performed? _16_

1. For each line:

    a) Name the Key.
    ___ b) Write the Root/Quality Chord Symbol above and the Functional Chord Symbol below.
    10

Root/Quality
Chord Symbol: B♭   C   F   C⁷

Key: F Major

Functional
Chord Symbol: IV   V   I   V⁷

Root/Quality
Chord Symbol: C   Fm   B♭m   C⁷

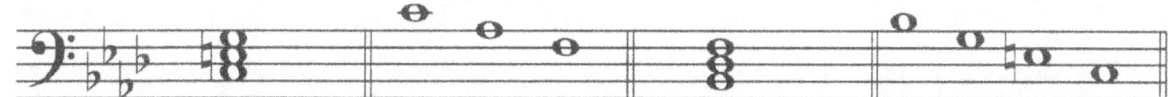

Key: f minor

Functional
Chord Symbol: V   i   iv   V⁷

2. Add rests below the brackets to complete each of the following measures.

10

3. a) Name the key of this melody.
    b) Draw a phrase mark (slur) over the given Question phrase. Label the scale degree number of the final note in the Question phrase.
    c) Compose a four-measure Answer phrase to create a Parallel Period. End on a stable scale degree. (There will be more than one correct answer.)
    d) Draw a phrase mark over the Answer phrase. Label the scale degree number of the final note.

—10

Key: Bb Major

4. Circle TRUE or FALSE for each of the following statements.

—10

a) TRUE or (FALSE:) Verse-Chorus Structure is used in the "Queen of the Night" Aria.

b) (TRUE) or FALSE: The "Queen of the Night" Aria is sung by a coloratura Soprano.

c) TRUE or (FALSE:) The emotion presented by the "Hallelujah Chorus" is sad and somber.

d) TRUE or (FALSE:) "Over the Rainbow" is sung by an SATB Chorus.

e) TRUE or (FALSE:) The Genre of "The Magic Flute" is an Oratorio.

f) TRUE or (FALSE:) The Genre of the "Messiah" is an Opera.

g) (TRUE) or FALSE: The text source of the "Messiah" is the Bible.

h) (TRUE) or FALSE: The Genre of the "Hallelujah Chorus" is a Chorus from an Oratorio.

i) TRUE or (FALSE:) An Oratorio is performed with dramatic acting, scenery and costumes.

j) (TRUE) or FALSE: The emotion (or character) presented in the "Queen of the Night" is vengeful and menacing.

5. Analyze this excerpt from the Menuet in G Major from the Little Clavier Book for W.F. Bach by answering the questions below.

a) Write the Time Signature directly on the music.

b) Mark the two four-measure phrases in this excerpt. Label them as a, a1 or b.

c) Explain the dynamic sign in measure 1. _play forte (loud), then play piano (soft) the second time when repeated_

d) Identify the interval at letter **A**. _Per 4_ . Identify the interval at letter **B**. _Maj 6_

e) Identify the Technical Degree Name of the note at: **C**: _Subdominant_ .

d) Identify the Technical Degree Name of the note at: **D**: _Dominant_ .

g) For the Triad at **E**, identify: Root: _C_   Quality: _Major_   Position: _1st inv_

h) Circle a recurrence of the rhythmic pattern at letter **F**.

i) For the Triad at **G**, identify: Root: _G_   Quality: _Major_   Position: _1st inv_

j) Explain the sign at **H**. _repeat sign - repeat the music_

1. a) Write the following Solid (Blocked) Triads or Chords in Root Position. Use a Key Signature and any necessary accidentals. Use whole notes. Write the Root/Quality Chord Symbol above and the Functional Chord Symbol below.

____
10

Dominant Seventh Chord of g minor.

Root/Quality Chord Symbol: D^7

Functional Chord Symbol: V^7

Subdominant Triad of G Major.

Root/Quality Chord Symbol: C

Functional Chord Symbol: IV

Tonic Triad of E flat Major.

Root/Quality Chord Symbol: E^b

Functional Chord Symbol: I

Dominant Triad of f minor.

Root/Quality Chord Symbol: C

Functional Chord Symbol: V

Subdominant Triad of f sharp minor.

Root/Quality Chord Symbol: Bm

Functional Chord Symbol: iv

Tonic Triad of b minor.

Root/Quality Chord Symbol: Bm

Functional Chord Symbol: i

b) For each of the following Dominant Seventh Chords, name the Key. Write the Root/Quality Chord Symbol above and the Functional Chord Symbol below.

Root/Quality Chord Symbol: F^7 C^7 D^7 E^7

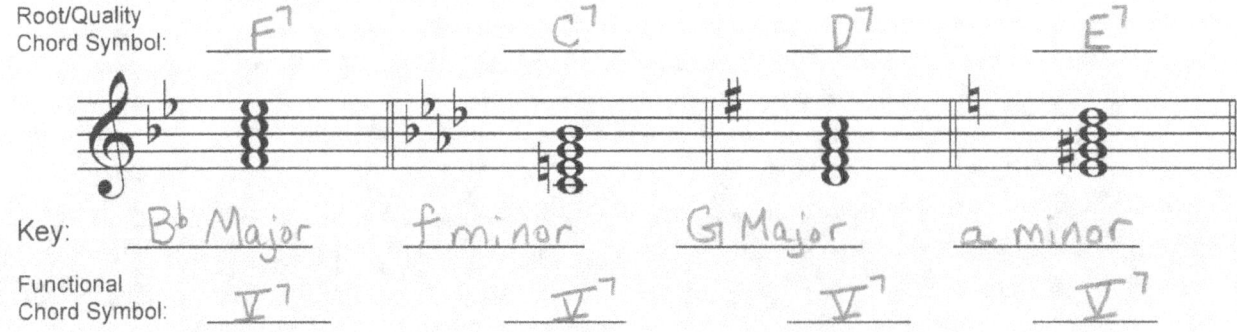

Key: B^b Major   f minor   G Major   a minor

Functional Chord Symbol: V^7 V^7 V^7 V^7

2. Draw one note that is equal in value to each of the following groups of notes.

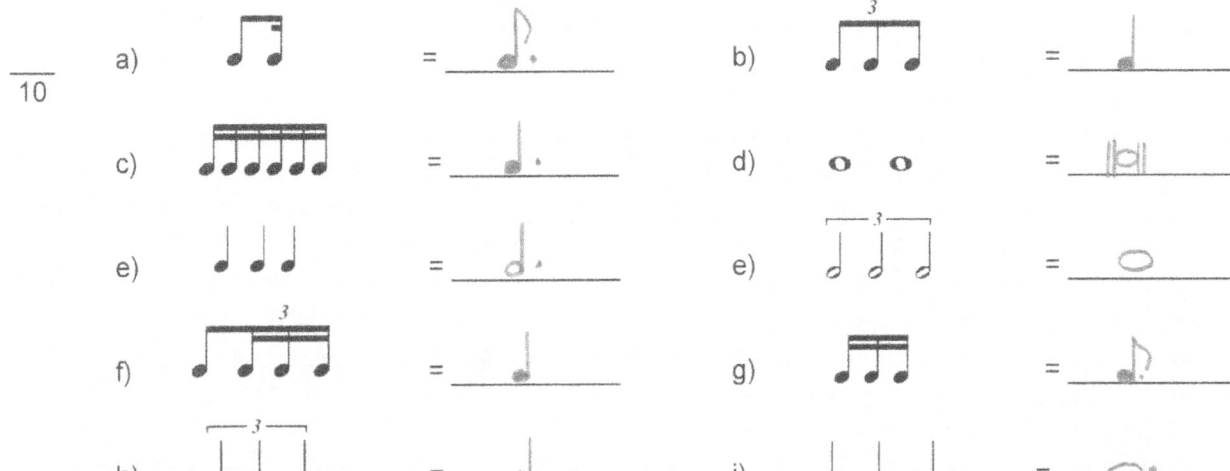

3. a) Write the note that is a Diatonic Half Step (Diatonic Semitone) above each note.

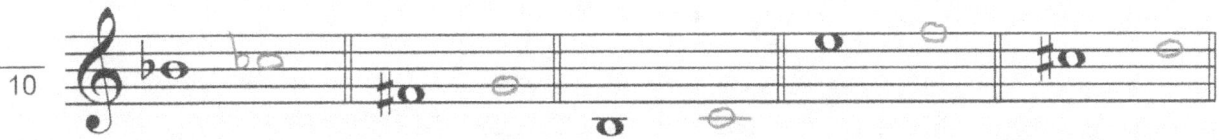

b) Write the note that is a Chromatic Half Step (Chromatic Semitone) below each note.

c) Write the note that is a Whole Step (Whole Tone) above each note.

d) Write the Enharmonic Equivalent for each note.

4. Name the scale. Write the scale, ascending and descending, using the correct Key Signature and any necessary accidentals for each. Use whole notes.

___ a) The Relative minor scale, melodic form, of E flat Major is: _C minor melodic._
10

b) The Parallel (Tonic) minor scale, harmonic form, of D Major is: _d minor harmonic_

c) The minor scale, natural form, with 4 sharps is: _c# minor natural_

d) The Major scale with 4 flats is: _Ab Major_

e) The Relative Major scale of f sharp minor is: _A Major_

5.   a) Add rests below the brackets to complete each of the following measures.

b) Add the correct Time Signature below each bracket to complete the following rhythms.

c) Add bar lines to complete the following rhythms. Add a double bar line at the end.

6.   a) Write the following Harmonic Intervals above each of the given notes. Use whole notes.

Major 2   minor 6   Perfect 5   Major 7   Perfect 8

b) Write the following Melodic Intervals above each of the given notes. Use half notes.

Perfect 1   Major 3   minor 7   Major 6   Perfect 4

c) Name the following Harmonic Intervals.

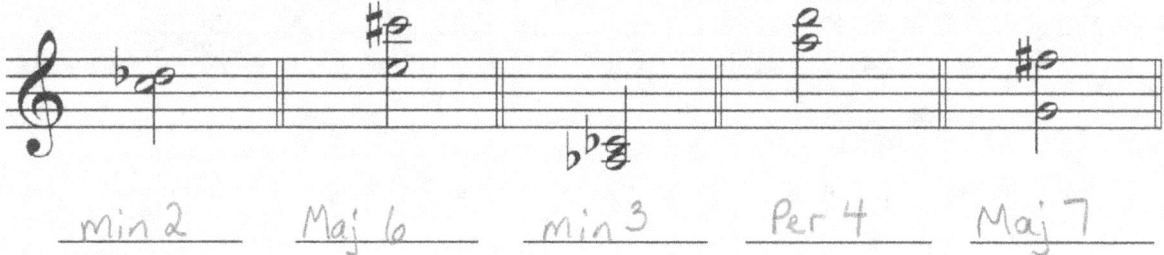

min 2   Maj 6   min 3   Per 4   Maj 7

d) Name the following Melodic Intervals.

min 6   Per 1   Maj 3   min 2   min 7

7.   a) Name the Key of the following melody. Transpose it up one octave in the Treble Clef.

Key: _f minor_

b) Name the Key of the following melody. Transpose it down one octave in the same Clef.

Key: _D Major_

8. a) Name the key of this melody.
    b) Draw a phrase mark over the given Question phrase. Label the scale degree number of the final note in the Question phrase.
    c) Compose a four-measure Answer phrase. End on a stable scale degree. (There will be more than one correct answer.)
    d) Draw a phrase mark over the Answer phrase. Label the scale degree number of the final note.

Key: **G Major**

b) For each Melody, mark the two four-measure phrases with a slur.
   Identify each phrase as a, a1 or b.

Melody 1:

Melody 2:

9.   Fill in the blanks to complete TEN (10) of the following statements.

___
10

a) _Messiah_ is an Oratorio composed by G. F. Handel.

b) _Harold Arlen_ is the Composer of "Over the Rainbow".

c) _Queen of the Night_ is an Aria from "The Magic Flute".

d) _W.A. Mozart_ is the Composer of "The Magic Flute".

e) A _Coloratura_ Soprano is a Soprano Voice with extreme agility and range.

f) The _Chorus_ is sung by Soprano, Alto, Tenor and Bass Voices.

g) The structure of "Over the Rainbow" is _Vocal with Verse-Chorus Structure_

h) The relationship between music and text is called _Word Painting_ .

i) The genre of "The Magic Flute" is _Opera_ .

j) W.A. Mozart was a composer from the _Classical_ Period.

k) Harold Arlen was a composer from the _20th Century_ Period.

l) G.F. Handel was a composer from the _Baroque_ Period.

Ultimate Music Theory
Level 5 Supplemental Bonus Exam

10.   Analyze the following by answer the questions below.

Minuet for Max

S. McKibbon-U'Ren

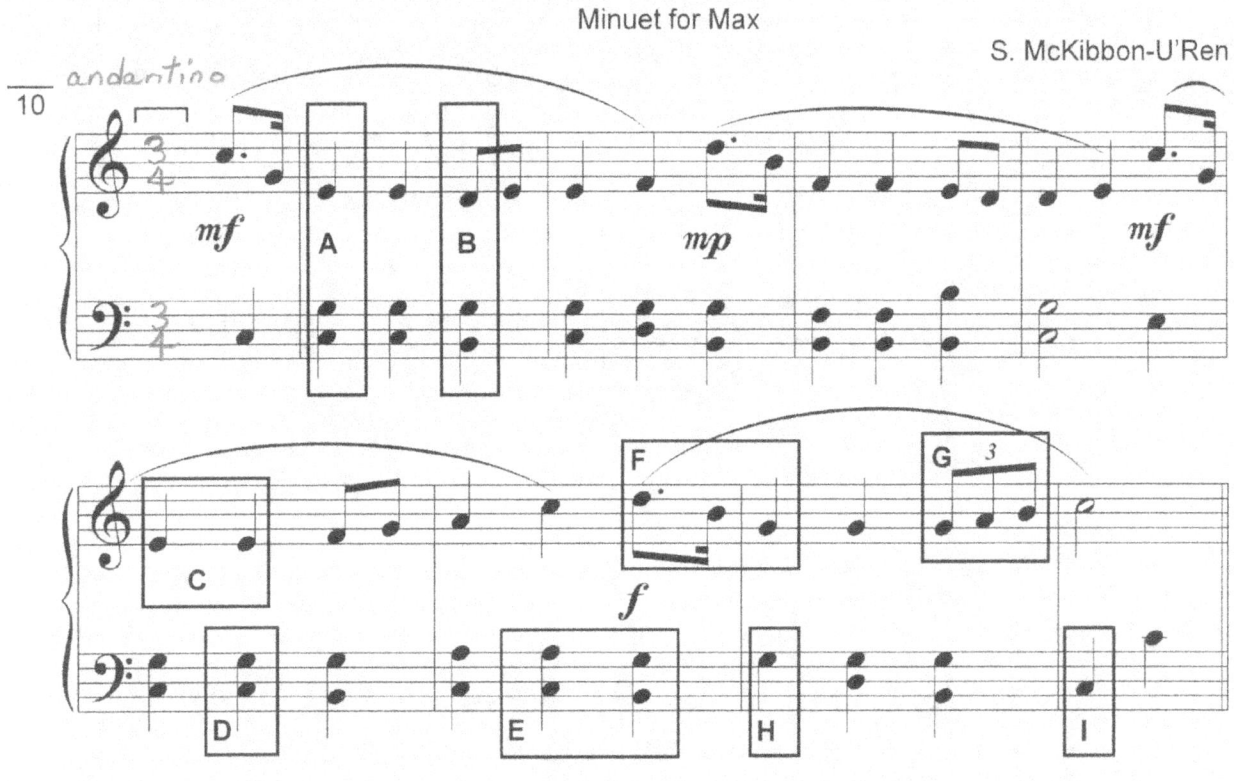

a) Write the Time Signature directly on the music.

b) Directly on the music, add a Tempo Mark indicating to play a little faster than andante.

c) For the Triad at **A**, identify: Root: _C_   Quality: _Major_   Position: _root pos_.

d) For the Triad at **B**, identify: Root: _G_   Quality: _Major_   Position: _1st inv_.

e) Identify the interval at letter **C**. _Per 1_. Identify the interval at letter **D**. _Per 5_.

d) Circle if the intervals at **E** are: Parallel 3rds   or   (Parallel 6ths)   or   Parallel 8ths.

g) For the Triad at **F**, identify: Root: _G_   Quality: _Major_   Position: _root pos_.

h) Identify the type of notes at **G**: _triplet 8th notes_.

i) Identify the Technical Degree Name of the notes at **H**: _Dominant_ **I**: _Tonic_.

j) For this piece, identify the: Number of slurs (phrases): _4_   Number of measures: _8_.

TOP 10 Ultimate Music Theory Tips
To Score 100% on Exams

Tip #1: Students should complete at least 8 Practice Examinations before writing their Final Exam. LEVEL 5 Exams will have one hour to be completed.

Tip #2: Hold a "Practice Examination" in your studio. Have all students who are writing their Exams come at the same time. They can only bring a ruler, eraser and pencil. Set a Timer. When the timer starts, the examination begins – no talking, no cell phones, no open books!

Tip #3: Pizza Party! On the night before their Examinations, have a "Pizza Party" – Use the Ultimate Music Theory Flashcards App, UMT Whiteboard and UMT Games to review terminology and concepts. Everyone will have fun and everything will be fresh in their minds.

Tip #4: On Exam day, Students should arrive 15 minutes before the start time of their Examination.

Tip #5: If the Student is not given a piece of blank paper to use to write out their UMT Map before beginning their Examination, they should ask for one from the Exam Center Representative. (Have your Student practice asking for a blank piece of paper.)

Tip #6: Remind both Student and Parent that it is the Student's responsibility to bring a mechanical pencil (with extra lead), or 2 - 3 pencils (with a pencil sharpener), eraser and ruler. They cannot bring any items that have "music" on them, so they cannot bring their UMT Rulers.

Tip #7: It is always a good idea to bring a tissue or two, a bottle of water and a couple of hard candies if it is cold/allergy time. Be sure to get plenty of rest the day before the exam.

Tip #8: Complete the exam in order beginning with question 1. Review what your Student can do if they get stuck – if their brain goes blank on a question. One suggestion would be to continue to the next question and then go back later to finish that question.

Tip #9: Remind Students to look at the front AND back of each page to ensure that ALL questions have been answered... and checked... and double checked.

Tip #10: Ultimate Music Theory 100% Club - *The Way to Score Success!* You and your student can become a member of the UMT 100% Club when your student receives a score of 100% on their nationally recognized theory exams including the RCM Theory Examinations.

Go to UltimateMusicTheory.com and complete the UMT 100% Club Form to receive your special 100% Club Certificate & Congratulations!

 **Workbooks, Exams, Answers, Online Courses, App & More!**

A Proven Step-by-Step System to Learn Theory Faster - from Beginner to Advanced.

Innovative techniques designed to develop a complete understanding of music theory, to enhance sight reading, ear training, creativity, composition and musical expression.

All UMT Series have matching Answer Books!

The UMT Rudiments Series - Beginner A, Beginner B, Beginner C, Prep 1, Prep 2, Basic, Intermediate, Advanced & Complete (All-In-One)

♪ 12 Lessons, Review Tests, and a Final Exam to develop confidence
♪ Music Theory Guide & Chart for fast and easy reference of theory concepts
♪ 80 Flashcards for fun drills to dramatically increase retention & comprehension

Rudiments Exam Series - Preparatory, Basic, Intermediate & Advanced

♪ 8 Exams plus UMT Tips on How to Score 100% on Theory Exams

Each Rudiments Workbook correlates to a Supplemental Workbook.

The UMT Supplemental Series - Prep Level, Level 1, Level 2, Level 3, Level 4, Level 5, Level 6, Level 7, Level 8 & Complete (All-In-One) Level

♪ Form & Analysis and Music History - Composers, Eras & Musical Styles
♪ Melody Writing using ICE - Imagine, Compose & Explore
♪ 12 Lessons, Review Tests, Final Exam and 80 Flashcards for quick study

Supplemental Exam Series - Level 5, Level 6, Level 7 & Level 8

♪ 8 Exams to successfully prepare for nationally recognized Theory Exams

UMT Online Courses, Music Theory App & More

♪ UMT Certification Course, Teachers Membership & Elite Educator Program
♪ Ultimate Music Theory App correlates to the Rudiments Workbooks
♪ Free Resources - Teachers Guide, Music Theory Blogs, videos & downloads

Go To: **UltimateMusicTheory.com**